Ten Things About

Revival
&
The Outpouring of
the Holy Spirit

Ten Things About

Revival
&
The Outpouring of the Holy Spirit

Reggie Weems

O LORD, I have heard the report of you,
and your work, O LORD, do I fear.
In the midst of the years revive it;
in the midst of the years make it known;
in wrath remember mercy.
Habakkuk 3:2

Restore us again, O God of our salvation,
and put away your indignation toward us!
Will you be angry with us forever?
Will you prolong your anger to all generations?
Will you not revive us again,
that your people may rejoice in you?
Show us your steadfast love, O LORD,
and grant us your salvation.
Psalm 85:4-7

You make known to me the path of life;
in your presence there is fullness of joy;
at your right hand are pleasures forevermore.
Psalm 16:11

Unless otherwise noted, Scripture quotations are taken from The Holy Bible, English Standard Version® (ESV®) Copyright © 2001 by Crossway, a publishing ministry of Good News Publishers. All rights reserved. ESV Text Edition: 2016

Copyright © 2018, Reggie Weems
www.10thingsabout.org

All rights reserved. No part of this book may be reproduced, scanned, or distributed in any printed or electronic form without permission.

First Edition: 2018

ISBN 978-0-9996559-5-5

To buy quantities of this book at a special rate for bulk use, email
info@greatwriting.org

Great Writing Publications
www.greatwriting.org
Taylors, SC

Table of Contents

About the Series and this Book 9

Introduction 10

1 Let's Define Revival 13

2 Revival in the Old Testament 20

3 Revival in the New Testament 25

4 Revival in Christian History 31

5 The Place of Prayer in Revival 37

6 The Need for Revival 42

7 Praying for Revival 49

8 The Cost of Revival 53

9 Concerns about Revival 69

10 After Revival 77

Conclusion 83

Appendix 86

About the Author 87

In memory of
Del Fehsenfeld
&
in honor of
Sammy Tippit, Steve Canfield,
&
Matt Fredericks

three generations of men
seeking God in revival

About the Series and this Book

TEN THINGS is a series of books offering biblical encouragement and practical direction on matters of concern to modern Christians who are seeking Bible-saturated, Christ-centered, Spirit-empowered, practical guidance. The series is published in an electronic and print format for quick, private, and easy access.

The books are brief and to the point, enabling readers to access immediate help and genuine hope for real-life situations. They are also written in a pastoral tone intended to shepherd hearts and minds toward Christ-centered, whole-life transformation.

This encouragement is not intended to and cannot replace personal pastoral counsel or the accountability of living transparently in Christian fellowship with other believers. Both are invaluable to you. A particular book may inspire a reader, but lifelong change only occurs in the context of living in biblical community.

Because of its biblical and simple approach, pastors may also employ the series to disciple church leaders who minister to God's flock.

Introduction

In 1971, twenty-four-year-old Del Fehsenfeld began Life Action ministries with the express purpose of seeking God for revival in America. Seven years later, God orchestrated a Life Action Summit at the church my wife was attending while I served the Air Force in a remote European assignment. A pre-planned month-long leave from the military ensured that I was placed in the midst of the region-wide revival that engaged innumerable churches and encompassed a three-month time frame.

The revival Teana and I experienced with Life Action revolutionized our individual lives and our marriage. It also provided us with a hunger for revival that remains with us today. For years, we have collected books and read about revival, praying for an outpouring of God's grace in our lives and in the churches of our ministry. And throughout the years, the Lord has been gracious to grant us glimpses of his glory. Thirty-nine years later, testimonies of God's saving and transforming grace still abound in Northeast Tennessee.

Life Action was my first experience with revival, a foreign word to me as a twenty-one-year-old airman. But my wife, who became a Christian at fourteen, had experienced the blessings of revival ministry several years earlier. Only a year after her conversion, Teana began attending Gateway Baptist Church in San Antonio, Texas, where Sammy Tippit was a member and itinerant evangelist. At that time, Sammy's ministry focused on serving Christ behind the Iron Curtain in countries where the gospel was forbidden and Christians were persecuted, even martyred for their faith. Sammy's ministry in those countries was everything Scripture and history spoke about revival; but he was experiencing it.

As a result of Sammy, Del, and the ministry of Life Action, God has graciously given us a glimpse of and thirst for revival—a passion that has only intensified throughout the years. We are grateful to God and the people whom the Lord has used to intensify our desire for him

It is imperative to study revival for several reasons. First, there is no reason for you to believe in or seek something that is not biblical. Second, reading about it may motivate you to seek revival. Third, studying revival demonstrates the means by which God grants this extraordinary visitation. Fourth, understanding revival protects you from deception. Fifth, knowing God's purposes for revival is all important.

This book is intended only as a primer. My hope is that God will use it to inflame your heart for revival. It is intentionally brief to encourage reading, and much of it is written in the first and second person to make it more conversational. Each chapter also has a section to help you meditate on and apply the principles of revival. In addition, I hope you will take advantage of the other books on revival listed in the Appendix.

1

Let's Define Revival

Repent therefore, and turn back, that your sins may be blotted out, that times of refreshing may come from the presence of the Lord. . .

Acts 3:19, 20

Jesus and his disciples made incredibly staggering promises; things like abundant life, rivers of living water, unspeakable joy, life abundantly exceeding anything you could ask for because it cannot be imagined. Picture bathing in a grace so deep and wide that anything else feels like something is missing. Visualize a clear conscience, a pure heart, an undivided mind, peace and wholeness – a life a life so perfectly aligned to divinity that it feels like you are surfing on omnipotence. What would you give, what would you exchange, what would you surrender for that kind of life? This is what revival promises and this is what revival delivers. It is a unique, life-transforming, supernaturally endowed experience like no other. And this is all true even though the word "revival" does not appear in the English Bible.[1]

---

[1] The words *revive* and *reviving* do occur. In the Old Testament (which is written in Hebrew), *revive* is from *chayah*, meaning "to live." It is used of restoring Jacob's

Nevertheless, "Revival is a church word: it has to do with God's people. You cannot revive the world; [just as] ….you cannot revive a corpse. But you can revitalize where there is life…."[2] That doesn't mean non-Christians aren't benefited by revival. Every historic revival has led to the conversion of innumerable people. But unbelievers are "dead in… trespasses and sins…" (Ephesians 2:1), and need resurrecting, not reviving. For Christians, revival is God's unique blessing for his glory among his people.

Defining revival can be difficult. Iain Murray astutely writes, "If we could understand revivals, they would not be the astonishing things which they are."[3] This is true. Revival reflects the infinite God who sovereignly chooses the if, who, when, where, how, and why of revival. Each revival in Scripture and

---

spirit (Genesis 45:27), of rebuilding Nehemiah's wall (Nehemiah 4:2), and of renewing Israel's health (Psalm 85:6). *Reviving* is from *michydh*, used as the restoration of Israel (Ezra 9:8-9). In the Septuagint, (the Greek translation of the Hebrew Old Testament) the Hebrew word *chayah* of Genesis 45:27 is translated as the Greek word, *anazopureo*, and in the New Testament (which is written in Greek), *anazopureo* is used of resuscitating Timothy's spiritual gift (2 Timothy 1:6). These verbs help provide a definition of *revival*.

[2] Quoted in Brian H. Edwards. *Revival: A People Saturated with God* (Darlington: Evangelical Press, 1990), 27.
[3] Iain H. Murray *Pentecost Today?* Banner of Truth 1998, 5

in extrabiblical history is as different as God chooses it to be. And yet, each is also similar, enabling us to arrive at helpful definitions.

A few quotes will help you to define and better understand revival. You will immediately notice one thing: "Almost as soon as you try to *define* the word revival, you find yourself *describing* what revival is."[4]

- *God's quickening visitation of his people, touching their hearts and deepening his work of grace in their hearts* — **J.I. Packer**
- *That strange and sovereign work of God in which He visits His own people, restoring, reanimating and releasing them into the fullness of His blessing* — **Stephen Olford**
- *Times of refreshing from the presence of the Lord* — **J. Edwin Orr**
- *An extraordinary movement of the Holy Spirit producing extraordinary results* — **Richard Owen Roberts**
- *A sovereign work of God's Holy Spirit that produces an unusual awakening of spiritual life among God's people, resulting in an awesome awareness of God, a sincere repentance for sin, a deep longing for God and holiness, and an effective passion to reach the unsaved* — **Brian H. Edwards**
- *A true revival means nothing less than a revo-*

---

[4] Edwards, *Revival*, 26.

> *lution; casting out the spirit of worldiness and selfishness, and making God and his life triumph in the heart and life* — **Andrew Murray**

In these contexts, revival is a unique, sovereign, powerful work of God in which he divinely restores the life of a Christian and church, even a nation, to the stature God intends; one that honors him, blesses people, and influences the world. It transforms subpar existence into supernatural living and enables you to live the life Jesus died to purchase. I define revival as

> *a sovereign work of God in which the Holy Spirit restores God's honor by reanimating the church's love for Jesus to its appropriate primacy and vigor.*

Or, as Vance Havner said, revival is "falling in love with Jesus all over again." My definition makes the subject of revival very personal. I hope you'll take it personally. Revival affects individuals, churches, and nations. But as the old hymn[5] rightly reminds us,

> *It's me, it's me, Oh Lord,*
> *Standing in the need of prayer.*

---

[5] From the hymn *Standing in the Need of Prayer*. Author unknown.

It is true that the word "revival" does not occur in Scripture. "But the teachings of Scripture go beyond its words. The Bible's ideas are full of revival theology, even though we cannot claim a certain biblical word as our warrant for a biblical concept of revival."[6] Even so, we may not be able to arrive at a single definition with which every Christian completely agrees. But this we know: "The wind blows where it wishes, and you hear its sound, but you do not know where it comes from or where it goes" (John 3:8). Revival is real and its effects are undeniable.

Before I ask you to desire, pray or prepare for revival, we must first establish that revival is a biblical concept. Extrabiblical history is replete with examples of revival but the Bible is our ultimate evidence for and guide concerning revival. Any expectation we have for revival must be rooted solely in Scripture. That's our discussion for the next two chapters. In the interim, take time to contemplate these thoughts.

---

[6] Raymond C. Ortlund, Jr. *When God Comes to Church: A Biblical Model for Revival Today* (Grand Rapids: Baker Books), 10.

Practical Application

1. How would you define revival?

2. Why is revival only for Christians?

3. What does God intend in revival?

4. Have you ever experienced revival, and if so, in what circumstances and with what results?

5. Do you see the need for revival in your life? In your church? In your nation?

2

Revival in the Old Testament

*As God, from the beginning has worked
prominently through revivals . . .
there can be no denial of the fact that revivals are a
part of the divine plan.*

E.M. Bounds

"Revival theology is pervasive in the Bible."[7] This is so much the case that there is a sense in which the history of Israel in the Old Testament can be read though the lens of revival.[8] The book of Judges serves as a summary and model of this Old Testament reality.

After entering the Promised Land, Israel loved and served God as long as Joshua lived (1:7). But when Joshua died (1:8), Israel broke their covenant with God by wicked living and idol worship (1:11-13). In response, God delivered Israel to their enemies. Israel's disobedience always resulted in the misery of multi-faceted defeat—spiritually, materially, economically and politically (1:14-17). When the judgment of God became unbearable, the nation repented and cried out to God (18b). God then raised up judges (the book of Judges oc-

---

[7] Ortlund, *When God Comes to Church*, 10.
[8] In his book, *Revive Us Again*, Walter Kaiser, Jr. lists eleven Old Testament revivals.

curred before the kings of Israel were established) who, in spite of their flaws, God used to rescue Israel. As a result, the revived people loved and served God but only for a season. This occurred seven times in the book of *Judges* and serves as a blueprint for revival in the Old Testament. It…

1. Occurred during spiritual and moral collapse
2. Began in the heart of a single person
3. Burdened someone to confess sin and beg for God's forgiveness and blessing
4. Was based on the preaching of God's Word
5. Promoted national repentance, confession and obedience to God's Word
6. Required the destruction of whatever challenged God's supremacy
7. Caused sin in any form to be forsaken for the love of God
8. Resulted in great joy and gladness

This is only one example of multiple revivals in the Old Testament. Sadly, Israel's failures in the book of Judges serve as a microcosm of the entire Old Testament. Yet if we are honest, Israel's story is ours. God has graciously saved us through Jesus' death, burial, resurrection, and exaltation. In response to that good news, God has turned our hearts to him, we have repented, forsaken sin, trusted Jesus as Savior, and pledged our obedience to God.

But inattention to that relationship or intentional sin has separated us from God, cooled our love for Jesus, and compromised our obedience. It's enough to make Jesus sick (Revelation 3:16). We have purposefully ignored or made excuses for our hard hearts but the reality is that we are no longer walking close enough to Jesus to hear his whisper, let alone lean on his breast and feel his heartbeat. The flame of our passion for Jesus has dwindled and is flickering. Sincere introspection will quickly detect evidence of this infidelity toward God. Consider these thoughts by way of practical application.

Practical Application

1. Would you classify your love for God and obedience to him as constant?

2. If not, what competes for your attention and affection?

3. Are you, right now, finding greater joy in any sin than in God?

4. If relational distance can be measured by a repentant heart, when was—and what was—the last sin you repented of and confessed to God?

5. What keeps you from confession and repentance?

6. Do you passionately fight to resist and eradicate sin in your life?

7. What godly attitudes and/or behaviors have you recently instituted to replace sinful thoughts and practices?

3

Revival in the New Testament

Christians in revival are accordingly found living in God's presence (Coram Deo), attending to His Word, feeling acute concern about sin and righteousness, rejoicing in the assurance of Christ's love and their own salvation, spontaneously constant in worship, and tirelessly active in witness and service, fueling these activities by praise and prayer.

J.I. Packer[9]

---

[9] http://graceonlinelibrary.org/church-ministry/revival/marks-of-revival-by-j-i-packer/ (accessed January 3, 2018).

Neither the noun in English for *revival* nor the verbs *revive* or *reviving* are found in the New Testament. The apostle Paul uses the word *revived* in the sense of the Philippians' renewed concern about him (4:10). But revival, as we are discussing it, is a New Testament concept.[10]

The sovereign, supernatural outpouring of the Holy Spirit at Pentecost inaugurated a new era. On that day, every Christian was filled with the Spirit, three thousand souls were converted, and the fear of God came upon believers and unbelievers alike. This isn't the twenty-first century norm. In this context, Pentecost is an historic and never-to-be-repeated event in the life of the church. Revival does not repeat Pentecost but it does present that same kind of extraordinary outpouring of the Holy Spirit's presence and power. This is because the Spirit was perma-

---

[10] In his book *Revive Us Again*, Walter Kaiser Jr. lists five New Testament revivals.

nently given to the church at Pentecost but you and I are not permanently filled with the Spirit. (We leak, to put it kindly.) So even though Pentecost will never occur again, it provided a model for revival that God has graciously chosen to grant the church in Scripture and history.

During his second stay in Ephesus, the apostle Paul received word that the Corinthian church was in trouble (1 Corinthians 1:11). The church was divided by personalities (1:10-12), enduring serious immorality (6:1ff), uncertainty about Christian marriage (7:1), food sacrificed to idols (8:1ff), spiritual gifts (12-14), and the resurrection (15:1ff). Don't let that succinct list mask the seriousness of the sin in Corinth. It was systemic, pervasive, enduring and publicly embarrassing to the gospel. This is why the Apostle's initial correspondence to the Corinthians (1 Corinthians) is direct and weighty.

But in his second letter, Paul acknowledges that the Holy Spirit had revived the Corinthian church (2 Corinthians 7:8-11). Godly sorrow moved the church to repent with *earnestness*, an eagerness to clear the church's name, *fear*, *desire*, and *zeal*. All of this led the people there to accept Paul's rebuke, acknowledge their sin, and passionately rehabilitate their individual and corporate life. This is congregational revival!

In Revelation, God rebukes five of seven churches for particular sins (2-3). Ephesus has left its first love. Pergamum entertains idol worshippers as members. Thyatira enables a false prophetess. Sardis is spiritually dead. Laodicea is lukewarm, wretched, miserable, poor, naked, and, worst of all, blind to its true spiritual condition. God called each church to repent of sin and return to him.

The message is clear: Revival is in the New Testament and God demands a revived church. We do not know how each congregation mentioned in the book of Revelation responded but we hope for a Corinthianlike revival. Regardless, God also calls you to revival which enables faithful Christian living. Think about the following aspects of the Corinthian revival and apply them to your own life.

Practical Application

When was the last time you experienced godly grief that moved you to repentance and renewed love for Jesus? Be aware, there is an ungodly grief.

"Godly grief," Paul writes, "produces a repentance that leads to salvation without regret…" (2 Corinthians 7:10). "Worldly grief," on the other hand, "produces death." Ungodly grief is sorry for the repercussions of sin. Godly grief is sorry for sin. Ungodly sorrow is emotional and without any transformation. Godly sorrow is both an emotion and action—a belief (my sin has offended God, hurt me and others), and behavior (God changes my life through the sorrow of my sin). Is the grief you experience over sin godly or ungodly?

The repentant Corinthian church was marked by earnestness to live for Christ publicly, indignation at their sin, fear of God and sin, a longing for the Lord, zeal for Jesus, and a willingness to endure the Spirit's conviction. Ask yourself these questions:

1. Do my friends and family know that I am a Christian?

2. What personal sin, if any, troubles me to the point of repentance?

3. How am I withdrawing from sin and drawing near to God?

4. What boundaries have I constructed to protect my relationship with Jesus?

5. In what particular ways do I give evidence of a passion for God?

4

Revival in Christian History

God, the Lord, came down amongst us.

George Whitefield [11]

---

[11] George Whitefield in Martyn Lloyd-Jones. *Revival* (Westchester: Crossway, 1987), 306.

Throughout post-Bible history, God has graciously revived the church. Here are just three examples.

For the first seven years of his Northampton, Massachusetts, pastorate, Jonathan Edwards applauded his congregation for its faithful attendance. But Edwards also complained that the people could not be awakened to spiritual matters. Dutiful to attend, the members were obviously distracted by worldly pursuits even as their pastor faithfully preached the gospel to them.

In 1734, God moved miraculously and mightily in Northampton. Matters of religion and eternity became of the utmost concern to Edwards' congregation and even to the town. Within a six-month span of time, Edwards counted 300 new believers and found the majority of people over sixteen were marvelously converted.[12] The church, Thomas Murphy

---

[12] Approximately 1,000 people lived in the town and 600 attended Edwards' church.

wrote, was "imbued with a life and energy that was irresistible."[13] Northampton quickly became the center of religious America, and Edwards, the nation's first celebrity. In a short time, revival spread throughout the Connecticut Valley and into all of New England, lasting from approximately 1740 to 1742. The church of God in America was revived and experienced what is commonly known as *The First Great Awakening*.

This American revival was accompanied by an equally great movement of God in England. There, George Whitefield and the Wesley brothers, John and Charles, are credited with saving a country on the verge of revolutionary terror, the likes of which decimated France (1789-1799). Wesley's "class meetings" asked methodical questions of its members, the most important question being, "Do you desire to flee from the wrath to come, and to be saved from your sins?" That reverential theme served as the DNA of the English revival. In 1928, Archbishop Davidson wrote that "Wesley practically changed the outlook and even the character of the English nation."[14]

The Welsh revival of 1904–05 began as a

---

[13] https://www.desiringgod.org/messages/jonathan-edwards-the-life-the-man-and-the-legacy (accessed December 18, 2017).

[14] Cited in Gene Fedele. *Heroes of the Faith* (Gainesville: Bridge-Logos Publishers, 2003), 165.

prayer revival expressed in the common cry, "I shall die unless God exerts his power and sends revival."[15] In 1901, Seth Joshua (1858–1925) walked the banks of the River Taff in Cardiff, crying, "God, give me Wales! God give me Wales!" At the same time, leaders from various denominations began unified prayer meetings for revival. In 1903, a week-long conference centered on praying for revival took place in Llandridod Wells. Another prayer gathering in August of 1904 ended with the unrehearsed, unrestrained, and repeated refrains of "Crown Him Lord of all!"

Earlier that year, Pastor Joseph Jenkins of New Quay at Cardigan Bay asked a catechism class of young people, "What does the Lord Jesus Christ mean to you?" A young girl responded, "I love the Lord Jesus with all of my heart." In the breathless silence that followed, weeping could be heard as the Holy Spirit graciously, gently but powerfully convicted many of the young people of their need for Christ. Jenkins reported that his church was revived with a passion for God. The movement spread as young people from his con-

---

[15] This overview of the Welsh revival and particularly the quotes not credited to James Stewart, are used by permission of David Pike. For a more in-depth review, see http://daibach-welldigger.blogspot.com/2015/08/the-welsh-revival-of-1904-5-overview.html (accessed 27 November, 2017).

gregation visited surrounding churches and towns sharing the good news of God's grace. It seemed a "spiritual cyclone"[16] was sweeping through Wales.

Before the end of 1905, it was reported that 100,000 people had been converted. Pubs closed on Sundays for lack of customers, soccer and rugby matches were canceled, and even courts were closed for lack of drunkenness and crime. Concert halls exchanged secular music for Christian music as the glory of God filled the theaters. One of the most humorous stories is that mules in the Welsh mines stopped obeying their masters because they could not understand the haulers' language without its normal profanities.

The Welsh revival can be summed up in the story of an American visitor who, arriving at a port, stopped a policeman to ask, "Where is the Welsh revival?" The policeman removed his hat, reverently bowed his head, covered his heart with his hand and replied, "In here." James Stewart writes: "The glorious fact and outstanding feature of the mighty awakening in Wales was that the sense of the Lord's presence was everywhere throughout the entire nation."[17]

---

[16] James A. Stewart. *Invasion of Wales By the Spirit through Even Roberts* by James A. Stewart (Asheville: Revival Literature, 1963, 2004), 50.
[17] Ibid., 38.

Practical Application

1. Ask yourself this question: "Do I desire to flee from the wrath to come, and to be saved from my sins?" (The "wrath to come" is God's judgment on anyone who does not repent of sin and place faith in Jesus as salvation from that wrath.)

2. What would it take for you to "flee from the wrath to come"?

3. Have you trusted Jesus Christ as your only and personal Savior?

4. When did this happen?

5. What evidences do you have that you are a Christian?

6. What would it take for you to be practically "saved" from the daily domination of your sins?

5

The Place of Prayer in Revival

Every mighty move of the Spirit of God has had its source in the prayer chamber.

E.M. Bounds

At forty-eight years of age, Jeremiah C. Lanphier resigned his fulltime job and accepted the position as a lay-missionary for the Old North Dutch Reformed Church, located on the northwest corner of Fulton and Williams streets in New York City (approximately two blocks east of the former World Trade Center). Lanphier immediately began inviting people from area neighborhoods to attend the declining congregation. After several discouraging weeks, he made use of handbills to advertise a Wednesday afternoon, 12–1pm prayer meeting.

On the first Wednesday, 23 September 1857, he was joined by six men from four differing denominations. Twenty men attended the second gathering, and forty the next. Encouraged by the increasing attendance, Lanphier boldly changed the prayer gathering to a weekday event. Within six months, 10,000 men daily gathered in about twenty prayer meetings throughout New York City. In the midst of every prayer meeting, people stood to publicly confess sin, repent, and entreat God's mercy. They also publicly confessed Christ as Savior. Lanphier's personal journal records 3,000 conversions within the first two months. The meetings grew so large so quickly that Lanphier established guidelines to maintain order and timeliness. People from other states and countries began visiting New York to attend the prayer meetings. Prayer requests from all over the world arrived in New York, and the mayor's office forwarded those addressed to Lanphier.

The prayer revival soon spread to Philadelphia where, on 8 March 1858, 300 people attended an initial prayer meeting. The next Wednesday, 2,500 people gathered in a larger auditorium. Within four months, it is estimated that 150,000 attended daily prayer meetings in a tent erected for that sole purpose. Within nine months, 10,000 people professed Christ in the city. The prayer revival then extended to Boston which influenced 150 Massachusetts towns to experience revival. Cleveland, Ohio, hosted a 2,000-person daily prayer meeting. Churches in St. Louis were filled to capacity for months. Later in the same year, the revival swept like a wildfire over the Appalachian Mountains and into the Midwest and the Pacific Coast.

A newspaper in Chicago reported on the 2,000-person prayer revival held in the

Metropolitan Theater in these words:

> So far as the effects of the present religious movement are concerned, they are apparent to all. They are to be seen in every walk of life, to be felt in every phase of society.
>
> The merchant, the farmer, the mechanic—all who have been within their influence—have been incited to better things; to a more orderly and honest way of life.
>
> All have been more or less influenced by this excitement.

By the end of 1858, the nation's churches had experienced a 10 percent increase in membership and it is estimated that between 300,000 and 1 million people were swept into the kingdom.

The 9 January, 1899 *Altoona Tribune* carried a very personal and moving obituary of the life and legacy of Jeremiah Lanphier.[18] His example is a powerful reminder of the power of prayer, and I encourage you to read it. Take a few moments to consider the existence and vitality of your own prayer life. Who knows what great things God will do for you?

---

[18] https://www.newspapers.com/clip/10476675/lanphier_jeremiah_c_death_jan_1899_ny/

Practical Application

1. On a scale of one to ten, with ten as the highest mark, how would you rate your prayer life?

2. Do you see the necessity or benefit of a faithful prayer life (talking to God)?

3. What does your prayer life look like?

4. Is it daily? Or is it only when difficulties arise?

5. What is the greatest hindrance to your prayer life? How could it be overcome?

6. Are you praying about your own spiritual health and growth?

7. Are you praying for God's blessing on your family, friends, church, and nation?

6

The Need for Revival

Revival is the visitation of God which brings to life Christians who have been sleeping and restores a deep sense of God's near presence and holiness. Thence springs a vivid sense of sin and a profound exercise of heart in repentance, praise, and love, with an evangelistic outflow.

J.I. Packer

Isaiah chapter six is widely regarded as an illustration of personal revival. The previous chapter is an indictment against Israel and news of God's impending judgment.

Verse 1a: Isaiah six opens with the death of Hezekiah, the man Isaiah expected to bring revival to Israel. Is all hope for revival lost?

Verse 1b: God reveals himself to Isaiah, exchanging the prophet's vision of Hezekiah for a view of himself. Since God is the "King of kings, and Lord of lords…" (1 Timothy 6:15), his throne is "high and lifted up," elevated above the earth. The size of the train on a monarch's robe demonstrates his wealth and power. As such, God's train "filled the temple."

Verse 2: Seraphim are angels whose name means "burning ones." They are burning with God's glory, the external manifestation of his holiness. Each seraph has six wings: two wings cover their faces from the burning glory of God; two to cover their feet as a demonstration of humility before God; and two wings enable them to fly because they cannot stand on such holy ground. (Think about Moses' feet-and-face encounters with God in Exodus 3:5 and Exodus 33:22.)

Verse 3: The seraphim cry, "Holy, holy, holy," because repetition represents exclamation points. "LORD of hosts," (which occurs 261 times in the Old Testament) points to God's "armies of heaven."

Verse 4: The greatness and power of God is demonstrated in the shaking foundations.

Verse 5: Isaiah was not an ungodly man. He was the national prophet of Israel. God spoke to him and he had spoken for God on many occasions. He had also witnessed God's holiness and power in the Lord's destruction of Sennacherib's army (2 Kings 19:35). Isaiah knew God in a unique way. Yet the personal, undiluted, one-to-one vision of God broke him. He recognized his sinfulness in the most dramatic terms—a confession that bears repeating and contemplation: "Woe is me! For I am lost; for I am a man of unclean lips, and I dwell in the midst of a people of unclean lips…"

Verses 6-7: God cleanses Isaiah with a "burning coal…from the altar." The cleansing removes Isaiah's guilt and atones for his sin.

Verses 8-13: God commissions Isaiah in an evangelistic ministry.

Isaiah's personal revival demonstrates our need for and the possibility of revival. If the national prophet of Israel—the man who regularly communed with God—discovered his need for revival, we are all in need of this grace.

Think about it. The average Christian doesn't intentionally set his or her face against God and seek to commit the most egregious sin possible in open rebellion to his revealed law. To my knowledge, no Christian is building an altar, buying a sacrifice, slaying it, and then offering it to an unknown, nonexistent god. But this doesn't mean we aren't idol worshippers. We daily exchange the immeasurable worth of God for people and things that aren't worthy of the attention or affection that are due God. And we are all guilty of undervaluing God and overvaluing the world.

It is what we consider respectable sins that most easily derail our intimacy with Jesus—the "little foxes [sins] that spoil the vineyards" (Song of Songs 2:15). It's also not only the things we do but the things that we don't do, perhaps inattention to certain things, that create the need for revival. Many sins are not those of commission but omission.

Use Isaiah's experience to apply the following list for personal reflection. Do any of these spiritually lethargic or sinful conditions reflect your present life and the need for revival?

- No passion to attend church
- No joy with church

- Boredom in church
- No conviction of sin in church
- No personal singing in church
- No desire for Christian fellowship at church
- No desire for Christian fellowship apart from the Sunday setting
- Refusing to submit to church leadership
- No financial support of the church and no service to the church
- No intimate, godly relationships
- Being unconcerned for God's glory in the church and the world
- A lack of concern for the lost
- Domineering
- Demanding
- Selfishness
- Critical
- Self-indulgent
- Overly self-conscious
- Unforgiving, blaming
- Unyielding
- Anger
- Bitterness
- Grudges
- Rejoicing about sin in your own life or that of others
- Married for selfish gain
- Marriage without eternal purposes and without ministry to each other
- Family without ministry to each other, children, and the world

- An absence of spiritual leadership in the home
- A lack of love for a wife, a lack of submission to a husband
- Attention to secular interests above spiritual disciplines
- Personal prayerlessness
- No weekday Bible study
- Private sin
- No community involvement for the sake of the gospel
- A lack of personal responsibility for your own spiritual maturation
- Decision making without reference to God
- A greater concern for children's secular activities than for their spiritual growth
- A toleration of gossip
- Jealousy
- A failure to confront sin in your own life
- A failure to confront sin in the lives of those you love
- An unwillingness to resolve relational conflicts insomuch as it is possible.[19]

Isaiah's personal encounter with God changed his life. Perhaps God will use the model found in Isaiah 6 to revive your life.

---

[19] This list is adapted and modified from *Seeking Him: Experiencing the Joy of Personal Revival* by Nancy Leigh Demoss and Tim Grissom (Chicago: Moody Publishers).

Practical Application

1. Ask God to give you a true vision of him in Scripture (Isaiah 6:1-4).

2. Ask him to search your heart about sin (Isaiah 6:5a; Psalm 139:23-24). (Use the list in this chapter as the basis of your reflection.)

3. Confess and repent of the slightest spiritual errors (Isaiah 6:5b).

4. Rejoice in God's abundant forgiveness (Isaiah 6:6-7).

5. Live in the sensitivity of that renewed relationship (Isaiah 6:8).

6. Obey God immediately and completely, and with a right heart attitude, regardless the cost (Isaiah 6:9f).

7

Praying for Revival

The spiritual disciplines of 2 Chronicles 7:14 are not just conditions for a true revival; they are the revival itself!

Lewis Drummond

There are two essential aspects to revival that balance God's divine prerogative and our human responsibility. Both sides are found in 2 Chronicles 29.

- Our responsibility—Then Hezekiah said, "You have now consecrated yourselves to the LORD" (v. 31).
- God's sovereignty—"And Hezekiah and all the people rejoiced because God had provided for the people, for the thing came about suddenly" (v. 36).

G. Campbell Morgan notes that a sailor has—and can have—no impact on the wind. But a good sailor knows the wind and understands how to set his sails for the wind. As Jesus stated, "The wind blows where it wishes, and you hear its sound, but you do not know where it comes from or where it goes" (John 3:8). Revival is a sovereign act of God. He chooses the time, place, and people to bless with an extraordinary measure of his

Spirit. It is true that you cannot create divine wind. But you can prepare your sails to catch God's wind. God is the Author. You can be his agent.

These texts demonstrate that we can and should prepare our hearts for revival.

Consecrate yourselves, for tomorrow the LORD will do wonders among you.— ***Joshua 3:5***

*For thus says the One who is high and lifted up, who inhabits eternity, whose name is Holy: "I dwell in the high and holy place, and also with him who is of a contrite and lowly spirit, to revive the spirit of the lowly, and to revive the heart of the contrite."—**Isaiah 57:15***

*Repent therefore, and turn back, that your sins may be blotted out, that times of refreshing may come from the presence of the Lord.—**Acts 3:19,20***

*Humble yourselves, therefore, under the mighty hand of God so that at the proper time he may exalt you.—**1 Peter 5:6***

2 Chronicles 7:14 is an often used text concerning revival. It reads, "If my people who are called by my name humble themselves,

and pray and seek my face and turn from their wicked ways, then I will hear from heaven and will forgive their sin and heal their land." According to this text, revival requires and produces

- humility,
- prayer,
- love and worship (seek my face), and
- repentance (turn from their wicked ways)

Even so, people cannot predict or produce revival. If it can be explained, it isn't supernatural. God is the sole source of revival, the sovereign work of a gracious God. Revival preparation is not a mechanistic formula intended to control a God who cannot be manipulated. It is not the result of planning or techniques. Nonetheless, the Holy Spirit makes us *response-able*—that is, able to respond to God's movement in our hearts. It is, after all, "God who works in you, *both* to will and to work for his good pleasure" (Philippians 2:13, emphasis added). Even though we can't create revival, there are things we can do to prepare our hearts for revival. Let's look more closely at that preparation, i.e., the cost of revival.

8

The Cost of Revival

We can come to the conclusion that we can do nothing for revival but pray. But I want to stress that there is more that we can do, namely that we must prepare the way by demonstrating to God that we are serious in wanting revival. There is no revival for those who do nothing and want nothing.

Brian H. Edwards

For me, this chapter is the heart of the book. There is no question that revival is biblical and historical. It doesn't need defending—only explaining. My assumption is that once revival is understood, every Christian will, of course, greatly desire the intimacy with Jesus uniquely produced by revival. Here are just five examples of how you can prepare your heart for revival.

Humility

"Humility" in 2 Chronicles 7:14 means "to subdue" as in bending the knee in reverence and surrender to God. Pride is the source and center of all sin. "EGO" is an acronym for *Edging God Out* of the center of our lives. In the English language, the letter "I" is at the center of PRIDE. Contrary to pride, humility is a life with God at its center. It is not simply a modest or low view of oneself. It is not meekness or weakness. Humility is the proper attitude toward oneself and others in relation to God. Peter's admonition to "Humble yourselves" is placed in the context of God's "mighty hand…" (1 Peter 5:6). "Mighty" means "ruling power" or "the ability to rule." God is mighty and we are not. Humility recognizes God as God and self as self, and then lives appropriately in the context of that reality and relationship. Peter's exhortation has an imperative meaning, "Do it now." As such, humility is your responsibility. It is your responsibility to know God and live in the weight of that divine gravity.

That reality changes the way we interact with other people who are also created in the image of God. Grace levels the living field for all humanity. Humble people do not put themselves first but others first. Humble people do not demand to be served but serve. Humble people are not fault-finders but, instead, they acknowledge fault. Humble people do not assert rights but yield rights. Humble people aren't easily offended but are concerned about offending others. Humble people live transparently instead of covertly. Humble people revel in grace, quickly acknowledging, confessing, and repenting of sin instead of exerting effort to cover it up or excuse it. Humble people follow the model of Jesus in Philippians 2:5-8 and, as a result, live uniquely Christian lives.

This is why the first element of revival in 2 Corinthians 7:14 is humility. Humble people pray. Proud people depend on self. Humble people seek God. Proud people live in a me-centric universe. Humble people turn from wickedness because they know it dishonors God and harms them. Proud people think sin advantages them without negative consequences. Humble people fulfill 2 Chronicles 7:14, and it humbles them all the more.

Prayer

In the Old Testament, David prayed for personal revival (Psalm 85:6) and Habakkuk prayed for national revival (Habakkuk 3:2). The word "pray" in 2 Chronicles 7:14 infers intercession; praying specifically for revival as a means of interceding for God's glory among his people and throughout the earth. God burdens his people to pray for revival, and Christians then passionately pray as the result of the divine burden. God hears that prayer and answers it in his sovereign will and joy. As such, prayer is both a vehicle to and a sign of revival.

Praying reveal attitudes and actions that are not commensurate with holiness. Broken Christians then repent of lives that grieve

(Ephesians 4:30) and quench (1 Thessalonians 5:19) the Holy Spirit. As Christians open their lives to the Lord and seek God's blessing, he pours out his Spirit in a fresh anointing which revives the church with a love for Jesus. The revived church then seeks God all the more, aligns its life to his will with laser focus, and God responds with a greater outpouring of his Spirit, both inside and outside the church. As James 4:8 wonderfully promises, "Draw near to God, and he will draw near to you." This is revival, and that intimacy becomes the new normal for Christian living.

As Christians seek God, he reveals his holiness, beauty, and power. This exposure results in humility, brokenness, concession, repentance, and joy. God blesses that revival of love for him with a greater revelation which, in turn, promotes deeper devotion by revived Christians. It is a circle of repeated revelation and repentance that ever widens and ever deepens.

Psalm 130 forms several easy-to-follow instructions for revival praying

- "The depths" of sin or sorrow establish the need for and ground of revival (vv. 1-2)
- Humility, confession and repentance generate and shape prayer (vv. 3-4)
- God alone becomes the focus of hope (v. 5)
- Revival becomes an all-encompassing passion (v. 6)

- That passion moves you to call others to pray (v. 7a)
- The character of God creates energy and hope for revival (vv. 7b-8)

Bible Reading, Study, and Application

The law of the LORD is perfect, reviving the soul; the testimony of the LORD is sure, making wise the simple. — **Psalm 19:7**

Christians are a people of *the* book. The Bible is the revelation of our irresistibly beautiful God. It is an essential element of revival for at least five reasons. It

- reveals revival: Without Scripture, we would not know that revival even exists;
- defines revival: Scripture tells us what to hope and pray for as we seek God;
- reveals its possibility: Biblical examples encourage us to seek God for revival;
- prescribes the prerequisites: Scripture directs us to essential disciplines;
- protects the church: Satan does create counterfeit movements;
- is God's reviving tool: Applying the Bible is what revives the church.

Each of the revivals under Hezekiah and Nehemiah were revivals of the Bible—reading and obeying it anew. Your relationship to the Bible is fundamental to your relationship to God. Prayer is how you communicate with God, and the Bible is how God communicates with you. He cannot be the center of your life if you do not make his word central to your life. Nor can you know what God requires of you, how to please him or what offends him, if you aren't reading the Bible.

According to 2 Timothy 3:16, the Bible is God's breath, as essential to your spiritual life as breathing is to your natural life. Simply put, the Old and New Testaments are your lungs. Without the Bible, your spiritual life will suffocate. The world's air is not sufficient for your spiritual life. Sometimes it is poisonous. On the other hand, God's Word will revive you; it will give you breath and life. It is oxygen to your soul and essential to revival. Look at the benefits of God's Word, as stated in 2 Timothy 3:16-17. The Bible

- clarifies what is right—"profitable for teaching";
- explains what is wrong—"reproof";
- shows how to put right what is wrong—"correction";
- teaches how to keep right, right—"training in righteousness".

An old saying rightly asserts "The Bible will keep you from sin or sin will keep you from the Bible." Scripture is essential in maintaining your relationship to God. It is God's voice to you. Your relationship to God will never be deeper, more intimate or more joyful than your relationship to the Bible. You should be reading it daily, memorizing it, meditating on it, and actively applying it to your life. An honest reflection of your life will require you to assess your relationship to Scripture, without which there can be no revival.

Repentance

Repentance is a combination of two Greek words: *meta* and *noeo*. The prefix, *meta*, means change, and *noeo* refers to the mind. In a Christian context, repentance means a change of heart and mind that results in a change of behavior that moves us toward God and Christlikeness. The younger prodigal mentioned in Luke 15 is an excellent example of repentance. He

- evidenced a change of mind "when he came to himself" (v. 17);
- evidenced a change of heart when he

said, "Father, I have sinned...before you" (v. 19);
- evidenced a change of behavior when "he arose and came to his father" (v. 20).

Scripture is very clear about the necessity of repentance. There is no gospel or Christianity without it. It is the first public word both John the Baptist and Jesus spoke as they began their ministries (Matthew 3:2; 4:17). Jesus summarized his ministry as calling "sinners to repentance" (Luke 5:32) and twice warned his listeners, "Unless you repent, you will all... perish" (Luke 13:3,5).

Like everything else about Christianity in general and revival in particular, repentance is a gift from God (Acts 11:18; 2 Timothy 2:24-25). This means repentance isn't natural to you. It is more likely that you will defend yourself, attempt to explain away your sin, or become angry if it is revealed. But you can ask God for repentance, and so you should. This is because repentance is a lifestyle and not a one-time or occasional act. We are repenting moment-by-moment, as the Holy Spirit convicts us about sin—as we recognize we have sinned or when someone lovingly points out our sin. Repentance is like a mid-course correction that you make each time you find yourself turning away from God's character, his word or his will. It is the unremitting renegotiation of your life toward the goal of conformity to Jesus. And it requires constant vigilance.

Repentance is made easier if you keep short sin-lists with God and short accounts with other people. This makes every attitude and action important. You must be intentional in your walk with Jesus. If you travel only 100 yards but go just one degree off course, you will miss your destination by 5.2 feet. That difference increases to 92.2 feet if you are traveling a mile. A one degree miscalculation on a trip to the moon means you would miss the moon by 4,169 miles, almost twice its diameter. If you are not intentional and live carelessly, you may unexpectedly find yourself missing God's will for your life. You cannot live the Christian life on autopilot. Repentance makes regular course corrections to ensure your life honors and reflects Jesus.

Let's change metaphors. If sin is a brick, each sinful thought, word, emotion or behavior works to build a wall between you and God and you and others. After days without repentance, a wall can exist between you and anyone you love. Marriages fail because sin builds walls between husbands and wives. This is one reason parents become estranged from children. Sin has this accumulating, multiplying, negative effect that can be demolished only by repentance. This is why the Bible compels you to not let the sun go down on your wrath (Ephesians 4:26). So be sure to keep a short sin-list with God. Keep small accounts with people. Every sin is a degree off course. Every sin is a brick. Don't let negligence build a wall between you and God or others. Repent immediately and regularly. As the apostle admonishes, "Let everyone who names the name of the Lord depart from iniquity" (2 Timothy 2:19).

Obedience

The repentant heart questions, "What then shall we do?" (Luke 3:10) and performs "deeds in keeping with...repentance" (Acts 26:20). None other than Jesus himself said, "If you love me, you will keep my commandments" (John 14:15). There is no room for misinterpretation in that statement and it doesn't leave any room for disobedience. This also makes obedience the acid test of love. "Whoever has my commandments and keeps them," Jesus says, "it is he who loves me" (John 14:21). God condemns heartless obedience (Isaiah 29:13). It isn't just obedience but heartfelt obedience that is required. Biblical obedience means obeying God immediately, completely, and with a right heart attitude.

Disobedience opens the door to the devil

and other temptations. There is simply no substitute for obedience. Partial or delayed obedience is disobedience. The matter of obedience and disobedience is the difference between building on rock and sand (Matthew 7:27-31). Jesus reminded his audience: "Blessed rather are those who hear the word of God and keep it!" (Luke 11:28). John exhorted his readers in these words: "Blessed are those who hear, and who keep what is written…" (Revelation 1:3).

God is not your copilot. He's your Creator, Savior, and Lord. Paul and Peter remind you that obedience is a matter of salvation and damnation (Romans 10:16; 2 Thessalonians 1:8; 1 Peter 4:17). If Jesus is not Lord, he could not have defeated death and sin. If he is not Lord, he could not save you. This means Lordship salvation is the only salvation.

Obeying the gospel also saves you daily from the world, yourself, and the devil. (The Christian term for this is *sanctification*.) Yet Jesus asks, "Why do you call me 'Lord, Lord,' and not do what I tell you?" (Luke 6:46). You and I don't get to choose the areas of obedience that suit us. Christianity is a radical call to holistic, comprehensive health made possible by denying oneself, taking up the cross (an instrument of death), and following Jesus (Matthew 16:24). Anything else is not Christianity.

As such, obedience speaks to the very core of our conversion. James counsels: "Be doers of the word, and not hearers only, deceiving yourselves" (James 1:22). What does he mean? Salvation assurance is sometimes inappropriately based on the memory of a one-time experience. Biblical assurance is grounded in present obedience. You know you are a Christian because you are a Christian today. This is because the grace of God teaches and enables you to say "no" to sin (Titus 2:11-12). Jesus warned, "Not everyone who says to me, 'Lord, Lord,' will enter the kingdom of heaven, but the one who does the will of my Father who is in heaven" (Matthew 7:21).

Del Fehsenfield, Jr. taught that "obedience brings blessing; disobedience results in conflict." You may be concerned that obedience is costly. It is. But disobedience is always costlier. You know it to be true biblically and personally. Noah obeyed God and it saved his family. Joshua's obedience won the battle of Jericho. Mary's obedience birthed Jesus. Jesus' obedience saved you.

Adam and Eve disobeyed, thrusting the cosmos into disarray. Lot's wife disobeyed and it cost her life. Abraham's partial obedience split his family and nations. Moses' disobedience kept him out of the Promised Land. Jonah's disobedience took him on a journey that he would never have anticipated.

You may say, "But it costs so much to love Jesus." It does. But I can assure you from the Bible, pastoral wisdom, and personal experience that any other love will cost you immeasurably more. Loving Jesus first and foremost is only appropriate. "In him is life" (John 14:6), "fullness of joy" and "pleasure forevermore" (Psalm 16:11), and apart from him is only eternal misery. God loved you first. He loves you most. No one and nothing else deserves your first love (1 John 4:19). No one else and nothing else can adequately reciprocate that love. Whatever it costs, love Jesus.

Practical Application

1. Read Philippians 2:5-8 and trace the steps of Jesus' humility.

2. How does the model of Jesus challenge your life?

3. Using 2 Chronicles 7:14 as a model, what evidences exist that you are humble?

4. What other elements of 2 Chronicles 7:14 could you use to cultivate humility in your life?

5. Does the Bible's revelation about revival encourage you to pray for it?

6. How can you construct a prayer life that regularly intercedes for revival?

7. What Bible verses could you use to pray for revival?

8. List the Scripture's requirements for revival to be seen in 2 Chronicles 7:14.

9. What does "repentance" mean?

10. Is repentance a regular part of your Christianity? How often do you repent of sin?

11. Why is repentance necessary for revival?

12. What command are you partially obeying? What command are you disobeying? What command have you yet to obey?

9

Concerns about Revival

O Holy Ghost, revival comes from Thee;
Send a revival, start the work in me;
Thy Word declares Thou wilt supply our need;
For blessings now, O Lord, I humbly plead.

J. Edwin Orr

No book about revival would be complete without appropriate warnings. Let's look at just four concerns.

Human Effort

Samuel Chadwick wrote, "The pretense of spirituality is the worst profanity.... The absence of reality is sad enough, but the aggravation of pretense is a deadly sin."[20] There are no substitutes for—and no shortcuts to— genuine revival. But people still try deadly alternatives. "Not everything called revival is revival. But authentic revival is a holy thing."[21] Nevertheless, many people aspire to build Babel instead of obeying God (Genesis 11:1-9). Scripture is littered with humanity's

---

[20] Samuel Chadwick. *The Way to Pentecost* (Fort Washington: CLC Publications, 2000, 2013), 15.
[21] Ortlund, *When God Comes to Church*, 20.

attempts to access God's power void of his Spirit. Satan often attempts to counterfeit divine work. God's miracles in Egypt were copied by Pharaoh's magicians (Exodus 11-12). Simon tried to buy the disciples' power (Acts 8:9-25). But our efforts can never duplicate God's omnipotence. And the Holy Spirit will never contradict God's authoritative word.

You must be discerning without being a skeptic. Revivalism is not revival. We can't schedule it. God cannot be domesticated to our timelines. And organizing does not replace agonizing. If the Holy Spirit is not honored in revival, it is not revival. And the end never justifies the means in any Christian endeavor. The real problem with human effort is that it often works but with terrible consequences; just ask Abraham. But only the Holy Spirit can effect lifelong, even eternal, transformation. Repeated attempts to mimic God's work only discourages Christians from seeking true revival. It also encourages people to trust in human effort with disastrous consequences (Matthew 12:43-45).

Revival for the Sake of Revival

"There can be nothing better on earth than a

true Holy Spirit revival…"[22] Because revival is so powerful, people may be tempted to seek it for its own sake. Revival is a magnificent experience but you should not seek revival as an end, in and of itself. Revival is a means to experiencing God—knowing, loving, and honoring him. Seeking revival for the sake of revival is idol worship. And seeking revival for your sake is another version of selfishness, which is antithetical to the gospel.

Satan very craftily takes good things and ever so slightly turns our hearts toward those things and away from the God who gives them. But "fullness of joy" and "pleasures forevermore" are available only from God (Psalm 16:11). Our flesh also conspires against us. It will often settle on a lesser joy, stopping short of God. We live in an experience-driven world but no experience and no feeling in the world can replace God. In this sense, revival could be defined as God's manifest presence. But don't mistake the experience or emotion felt in revival for God himself. God sends revival to revive the glory of his name, for the joy of his people, and the gospel in the world—not to satisfy carnal desires.

---

[22] Edwards, *Revival*, 15.

Anti-Revivalism

Revival is sometimes misunderstood and, as a result, opposed by well-meaning, sincere Christians. The church often falls into one of two extremes: considering every movement a revival or denying that any movement is revival. But revival is a biblically supported marvel. In 1990, my English friend, Brian H. Edwards, wrote *Revival: A People Saturated with God*. British Christians responded with concerns that revival is just a church phenomenon without biblical support. As such, Brian felt compelled to write a further work titled, *Can We Pray for Revival?*

Every genuine revival also provokes an anti-revival spirit. Perhaps the most infamous enemies of revival in the Old Testament are Ahab and his wife, Jezebel. Ahab "did evil in the sight of the LORD, more than all who were before him" (1 Kings 16:30). He even accused Elijah of evil (1 Kings 18:17) but the king himself was God's real enemy. When Nehemiah led Israel to rebuild the walls of Jerusalem, Sanballat repeatedly undermined those efforts (Nehemiah chapter 2 onwards). He was "angry, greatly enraged, and he jeered at the Jews" hoping to discourage them (Nehemiah

4:1). When that did not work, he proposed five peace gatherings that were actually covert attempts to harm Nehemiah (6:2-4). When that failed, he lied about the Jews' intentions to the king (6:5-7). Sanballat ultimately tried to assassinate Nehemiah (6:10). Once the wall was completed, another enemy of revival, Tobiah, "sent letters to harass and terrorize" God's revived remnant (6:19).

Satan's Efforts to Oppose Revival

Satan will not be idle while God's people seek the face and blessing of God. Revival is spiritual warfare. Pursuing it will set the flesh, the world, and the devil against you. Pursuing revival places a target on your back. If you seek revival, the devil will begin an assault against your private life, marriage, family, work, church, relationships—literally everything about you. Temptations will multiply. Your schedule will fall apart. Work will become especially stressful. Your marriage will be tested. It will seem like anything that can go wrong will go wrong to oppose your heartfelt devotion toward God in revival. You will become hypersensitive. Little things—even meaningless things—will become gargantuan occasions for sinful thoughts, emotions, and behaviors. An unforgiving spirit, anger, and bitterness will attempt to lodge themselves in your heart. If you are not spiritually aware (1 Peter 5:8a), you will fall prey to frustrations that evoke responses that move you away from—not toward—revival, even as you pursue it. As you seek revival, you will face your own cynics or opponents. But your hope is in God alone.

When Jesus set his face toward Jerusalem and Calvary, one of his most trusted friends, Peter, rebuked him (Matthew 16:22). Likewise, you will not set your face toward revival without resistance. Your "old self" may become your greatest enemy (Ephesians 4:22). Others will also test your commitment. Once you start seeking revival, you must prepare your life for the devil's onslaught. This means you, as Paul warned the revived Corinthian church, cannot be "ignorant of his designs" or "outwitted by Satan" (2 Corinthians 2:11). I'm not encouraging you to see a demon behind every tree. But I am telling you that you must "be sober-minded; be watchful. Your adversary the devil prowls around like a roaring lion, seeking someone to devour" (1 Peter 5:8). This is never truer than when you become passionate about revival.

Practical Application

1. What is the difference between a revival God sends and a "revival" people create?

2. What about revival might cause people to see it for its own sake?

3. Why might people, even sincere Christians, oppose revival?

4. Why does Satan oppose revival?

10

After Revival

Revival is falling in love with Jesus all over again.

Vance Havner

By its very nature, revival doesn't last. It is "seasonal, not perennial."[23] Our feet get dirtied as we walk in the world and are in need of regular cleansing, even reviving (John 13:10). Revival reminds us of the holiness required to know and walk with God (Hebrews 12:4). It is also necessary because of the never-ending contest for our attention and affection. We fail to love God appropriately and revival reanimates our love for God (Deuteronomy 6:5; Mark 12:30).

Those who become Christians as a result of revival can join a local church, follow the Lord in believers' baptism, read Scripture daily, establish a prayer life, serve the cause of Christ in the church and the community, become generous givers, create spiritually based relationships, establish a godly home, and witness to those yet to be saved.

"God does not expect his church to be in continuous revival, but revival reveals those

---

[23] Ortlund, *When God Comes to Church*, 9.

ingredients God expects always to be present."[24] If your life is revived, you can seek to employ the passion of revival in practical disciplines that maintain your spiritual life and even increase your love for Jesus. Disciplines don't deliver revival but disciplines seek God for revival and are the result of revival. Here are a few disciplines to consider:

- Read your Bible every day and practice what it teaches;
- Obey the Holy Spirit immediately and completely;
- Keep a short sin-list with God;
- Be humble before God and with people;
- Confess when necessary;
- Repent immediately and wholly;
- Don't let people hinder your view of and love for God;
- Change your behavior. One aspect of the fruit of the Spirit is self-control (Galatians 5:23). I'm not advocating moralism (doing better without Jesus); I'm advocating Spirit-filled living.
- Put off the "old man" and put on the "new man" moment by moment (Ephesians 4:17-24);
- Keep a short account with family and friends;

---

[24] Edwards, *Revival*, 236.

- Don't let the sun go down on your wrath with anyone;
- Forgive immediately and completely. God commands this because he loves you and you aren't built to nurture an unforgiving spirit. It will consume your happiness. Even if people refuse to reconcile with you, on your part be reconciled with them.
- Lead by serving;
- Don't entertain temptation;
- Don't set any ungodly thing before your eyes;
- Keep your heart focused on Jesus and not others;
- Control your words;
- Use your time wisely for God-honoring pursuits[25]

Ephesians 4:17-32 provides an excellent blueprint for living the revived life. It centers on putting off "your old self" and putting on "the new self" (vv. 22-24). You can read those two sections of Scripture for a description of those two lives. The "new self" life requires constant vigilance, following Christ in

---

[25] There are many and valuable lists of pre-revival and post-revival disciplines / characteristics. Nancy Leigh DeMoss and Tim Grissom have an excellent list in their book *Seeking Him: Experiencing the Joy of Personal Revival* (Chicago: Moody Publishers).

obedience to the word, and repenting immediately and wholly as is necessary. I suspect everything essential to living appropriately before God can be summed up in the two phrases: "Do not grieve the Holy Spirit of God" (Ephesians 4:30) which could be interpreted as sins of commission, and "Do not quench the Spirit" (1 Thessalonians 5:19) which could be understood as sins of omission.

Practical Application

1. Why doesn't revival remain?

2. What Christian disciplines should be exercised by a new believer?

3. Looking at the list in this chapter, what disciplines should you begin practicing?

4. What attitudes or behaviors are you presently demonstrating that don't evidence a desire for revival?

Conclusion

The sea is out and I cannot bring a wind and cause it to flow again: Only I wait on the shore till the Lord sends a full sea.

Samuel Rutherford

In her biography of Andrew Murray, Leona Choy recounts Andrew Murray Sr.'s thirty-six-year "sacred Friday evening habit: he regularly devoted the whole time to praying for revival. He would shut himself in his study and read accounts of former revivals in Scotland and other countries, and often read stories to the family of the outpouring of the Holy Spirit on some particular church. Andrew vividly remembered standing outside the study door listening to his father's loud crying to God and pleading for a similar outpouring in his own parish, elsewhere in South Africa, and in the world."[26]

Revival is a sovereign work of God. Because it is divine in origin and supernatural in nature, there is much about it that cannot be explained. But it is biblical and, throughout Christian history, God has been pleased to bless the church with revival. Like Andrew

---

[26] Leona Choy. *Andrew Murray: Apostle of Abiding Love* (Fort Washington: Christian Literature Crusade, 1978), 27.

Murray, you can and should intentionally pursue it. Remember that I define revival as *a sovereign work of God in which the Holy Spirit restores God's honor by reanimating the church's love for Jesus to its appropriate primacy and vigor.* Revival is a matter of restoring God's honor, glory, and name by the church loving Jesus first (*primacy*) and foremost (*vigor*). That revived love then spills over into the world desperately in need of the gospel. Loving anything else first or foremost is idol worship, and idols are false gods, failed mechanisms for human health and flourishing.

Remember that this book is intended only as an introduction to the subject of revival. It is intentionally brief so as to encourage reading. My accompanying prayer is that God will stir your heart for revival and that, as a consequence, you will pray for, study about, and live in expectation of revival. If so, like grains of sand on the shore, you will join innumerable others, anxiously waiting in constant vigil for the tidal wave of sovereign grace to draw us into unfathomable oceans of revival.

> *But as for me, I will look to the LORD;*
> *I will wait for the God of my salvation;*
> *my God will hear me.*
> ***(Micah 7:7)***

Appendix

Discernment is essential for Christian living. This is also true of revival. I recommend the following books for their biblical faithfulness and ease of reading.

- DeMoss, Nancy Leigh and Tim Grissom. *Seeking Him: Experiencing the Joy of Personal Revival.* Moody Publishers.
- Edwards, Brian. *Revival: A People Saturated with God.* Evangelical Press.
- Lloyd-Jones, Martyn. *Revival.* Crossway.
- Kaiser, Walter C. Jr. *Revive Us Again: Your Wakeup Call for Spiritual Renewal.* Christian Focus Publications.
- Olford, Stephen F. *Lord, Open the Heavens!: A Heart-Cry for Revival.* Harold Shaw Publishers.
- Ortlund, Raymond C, Jr. *When God Comes to Church: A Biblical Model for Revival Today.* Baker Books.
- Ravenhill, Leonard. *Why Revival Tarries.* Bethany House Publishers.

About the Author

REGGIE WEEMS is married to his childhood sweetheart, Teana. They share three children and nine grandchildren. He has pastored two congregations: the first for ten years and the second since 1991. He also teaches theology, Bible, and humanities at two universities. His DMin in Pastoral Leadership and Management is from Liberty University, and his PhD in Historical Theology is from the University of Babes-Bolyai in Cluj-Napoca, Romania.

www.10thingsabout.org

To buy quantities of this book at a special rate for bulk use, email
info@greatwriting.org

www.ingramcontent.com/pod-product-compliance
Lightning Source LLC
Chambersburg PA
CBHW070548300426
44113CB00011B/1830